flower festival

50 Appliqué Blocks to Grow Your Garden ∗ 9 Quilt Projects

Kim Schaefer

C&T PUBLISHING

Text copyright © 2009 by Kim Schaefer

Artwork copyright © 2009 by C&T Publishing, Inc.

Publisher: Amy Marson

Creative Director: Gailen Runge

Editors: Lynn Koolish and Cynthia Bix

Technical Editors: Carolyn Aune and Helen Frost

Copyeditor/Proofreader: Wordfirm Inc.

Cover & Book Designer: Christina D. Jarumay

Page Layout Artist: Rose Sheifer-Wright

Production Coordinator: Tim Manibusan

Illustrator: Tim Manibusan

Photography by Luke Mulks and Diane Pedersen of
C&T Publishing, Inc., unless otherwise noted

Published by C&T Publishing, Inc., P.O. Box 1456, Lafayette, CA 94549

Library of Congress Cataloging-in-Publication Data

Schaefer, Kim,

 Flower festival : 50 appliqué blocks to grow your garden : 9 quilt projects / Kim Schaefer.

 p. cm.

 Summary: "50 blocks and 9 pieced and appliquéd quilt projects in a colorful, contemporary folk-art appliqué style"--Provided by publisher.

 ISBN 978-1-57120-529-2 (paper trade : alk. paper)

 1. Appliqué--Patterns. 2. Patchwork--Patterns. 3. Flowers in art. I. Title.

 TT779.S33 2009

 746.44'5041--dc22

                          2008024013

Printed in China

9 8 7 6 5 4 3

dedication

To my Mom, who always loved her garden.

acknowledgments

I am so fortunate to work with C&T Publishing. Everyone there has been supportive, encouraging, and a pleasure to work with. Thanks to all of you. I would especially like to thank Lynn Koolish, and Cynthia Bix, my editors, who have made the whole process easy and rewarding.

Thanks to Carolyn Aune and Helen Frost, my technical editors. I am grateful to have them checking my work. Technical editing is such a hard job, and they are so great at it. Thanks to the very talented Christina Jarumay for the book's great cover and design. Thanks to Tim Manibusan for the fine illustrations.

Thanks to Julie and the staff at Patched Works, Inc., for their support and for the original and creative longarm quilting. Thanks also to Lynn Helmke for the beautiful longarm quilting.

I would also like to thank my husband, Gary, for his continued support and for transcribing my book to disc.

Finally, I would like to thank my mom, Alice Sanders, for instilling in me a love of the garden. Although I have surrendered my garden to the deer, I try to capture the beauty of the garden and bring it inside with my quilts.

contents

introduction

T he garden theme has always been a favorite of mine, as it is for quilters everywhere. In this book you will find 50 different garden-themed blocks that finish to 8" × 8". If you want to change the size of the blocks for your quilt, simply enlarge or reduce the design using a photocopier.

I've also included a variety of projects to showcase your blocks, including table runners, table toppers, wall quilts, lap quilts, and single-block quilts. All of these projects are perfect for gift giving.

I hope that you will use the blocks in this book as an inspiration and a starting point to make your own quilts. Feel free to mix and match the blocks, or choose one or more of your favorites. The possibilities are endless.

general instructions

ROTARY CUTTING

I cut all the fabrics used in the pieced blocks, borders, and bindings with a rotary cutter, an acrylic ruler, and a mat. I trimmed the blocks and borders with these tools as well.

PIECING

All measurements for piecing include ¼" seam allowances. If you sew an accurate ¼" seam, you will have happiness, joy, and success in quilting. If you don't, you will have misery, tears, and the seam ripper.

 tip

> My best quilt-making tip is: Learn to sew an accurate ¹/₄" seam.

PRESSING

Press seams to one side, preferably toward the darker fabric. Press and lift the iron. Avoid sliding it over the pieces, which can distort and stretch them. To reduce bulk when you join two seamed sections, press the seams in opposite directions so they nest together.

APPLIQUÉ

All appliqué instructions are for fusible web with machine appliqué, and the appliqué patterns have been drawn in reverse. If you prefer a different appliqué method, you will need to trace a mirror image of the pattern and add seam allowances to the appliqué pieces.

A lightweight paper-backed fusible web works best for machine appliqué. Choose your favorite fusible web, and follow the manufacturer's directions.

General Appliqué Instructions

1. Trace all parts of the appliqué design on the paper side of the fusible web. Trace each layer of the design separately. For example, trace all the petals on a flower as one piece, and trace the center as another. Whenever two shapes in the design butt together, overlap them by about ⅛" to help prevent the potential for a gap between them. When tracing the shapes, extend the underlapped edge ⅛" beyond the drawn edge in the pattern. Write the pattern letter or number on each traced shape.

2. Cut around the appliqué shapes, leaving a ¼" margin around each one.

3. Iron each fusible web shape to the wrong side of the appropriate fabric, following the manufacturer's instructions for fusing. Cut on the tracing lines, and peel the paper backing off the fusible web. A thin layer of fusible web will remain on the wrong side of the fabric—this layer will adhere the appliqué pieces to the backgrounds.

4. Position the pieces on the backgrounds. Press to fuse them in place.

5. Machine stitch around the appliqué pieces using a zigzag, satin, or blanket stitch. Stitch any detail lines indicated on the patterns.

My choice is the satin stitch. I generally use beige thread for all the stitching. Sometimes the stitches blend with the fabric, and sometimes they don't. Using one color throughout gives the quilt a folk art look. However, on the *Tulip Lap Quilt* (page 81), I used black thread, and you can see how changing the thread color changed the entire look of the quilt. As always, the type of stitching you use and the thread color you select are personal choices.

PUTTING IT ALL TOGETHER

When you've completed all the blocks for a quilt, lay them out on the floor or, if you're lucky enough to have one, a design wall. Arrange and rearrange the blocks until you are happy with the overall look of the quilt top. Each project has specific directions, as well as diagrams and photos, for assembling the top.

BORDERS

All borders in the book are straight cut with no mitered corners. This technique enhances the quilts' folk look, and it's easier and faster as well. Join border strips at a 45° angle, as necessary, to achieve the desired length.

LAYERING THE QUILT

Cut the batting and backing pieces 2″ to 3″ larger than the quilt top on each side for table runners and smaller quilts (less than 40″) and 3″ to 4″ larger on each side for larger quilts. (If you are planning on having the piece quilted by a longarm quilter, check with your quilter for specific requirements.) Place the pressed backing on a flat surface, with the right side facing down. Place the batting over the backing, and then place the quilt top on the batting. Make sure that everything is flat and smooth and that the quilt top is centered over the batting and backing. Pin or baste the layers together.

QUILTING

Quilting your quilt is a personal choice; you may prefer hand or machine quilting. I like to send my quilts to a longarm quilter. This method keeps my number of unfinished quilt tops low and my number of finished quilts high.

COLOR AND FABRIC CHOICES

I am a scrap quilter, and I have a very relaxed approach to color and fabric choice. If I like it, I use it. Scrap quilting lends itself well to this approach. Generally the more fabrics I use, the more I like the quilt. I must confess, however, that I am not opposed to buying new "scraps." If I have a color theme in mind for a quilt, as in the *Tulip Lap Quilt* (page 81) or the *Splash Lap Quilt* (page 77), and I don't have enough of these colors in my stash, I buy them. I guess it could be argued that technically these aren't scraps; however, they do give the quilt a scrappy look. In the end, it is your quilt and your choice, and if you're happy, that's what's important. All the fabrics I use are 100% cotton.

YARDAGE AND FABRIC REQUIREMENTS

Most of the fabric manufacturers print 100% cotton in widths that range from 40″ to 44″. Because of this variance, all the fabric requirements in this book were calculated based on a 40″ width.

I have given yardage and fabric requirements for each project, with many listings calling for a total amount of assorted fabrics that can be used as a base for your quilt. The yardage amounts vary depending on the size of the quilt, the number of fabrics used, and the number of pieces you cut from each fabric. I don't worry about running out of a particular fabric. For a scrappy look, the more different fabrics there are, the better.

I prefer to use the lengthwise grain of the fabric for quilt backings, even on smaller projects. For larger quilts, I piece together two or three lengths of fabric.

Fabric amounts for bindings allow for 2″-wide strips cut on the straight of grain. Fusible web amounts are based on a 17″ width.

FLOWER FESTIVAL

the blocks

2

3

+

5
4

1

7

6

#1 Sunflower

#2 Checker Bloom

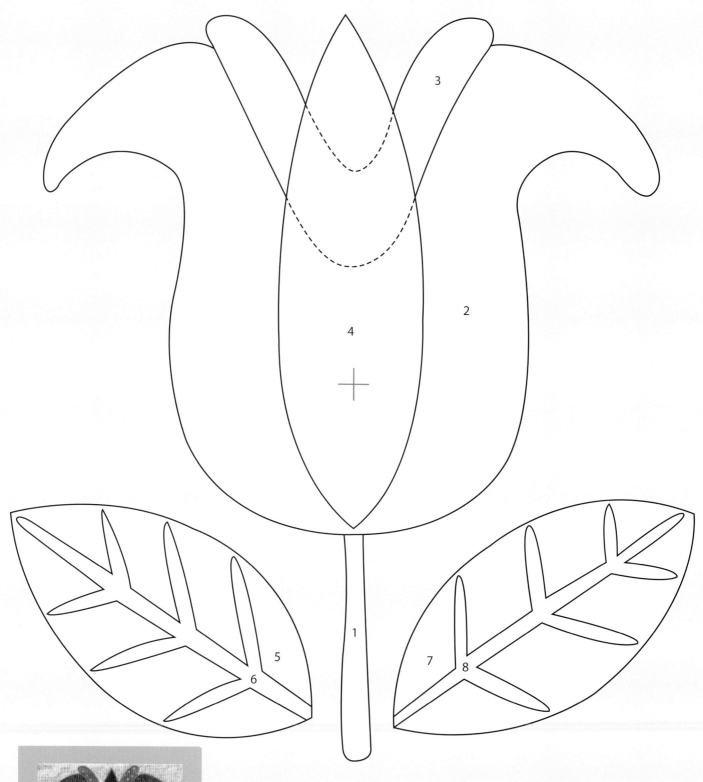

3

2

4

+

1

5

6

7

8

#3 Dutch Delight

FLOWER FESTIVAL

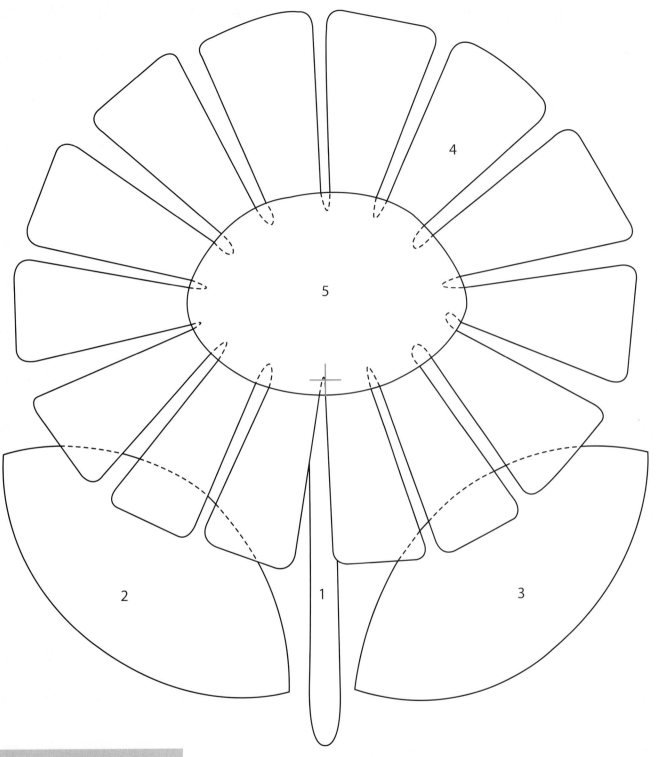

4

5

2

1

3

#4 Dazzle Daisy

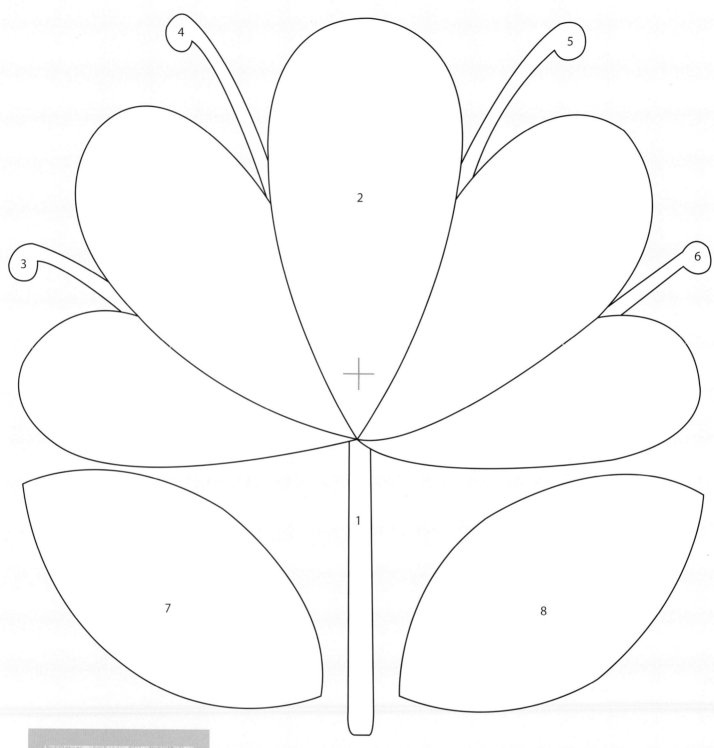

4

5

3

6

2

+

1

7

8

#5 Moon Flower

4

5

6

2   1   3

#6 Morning Star

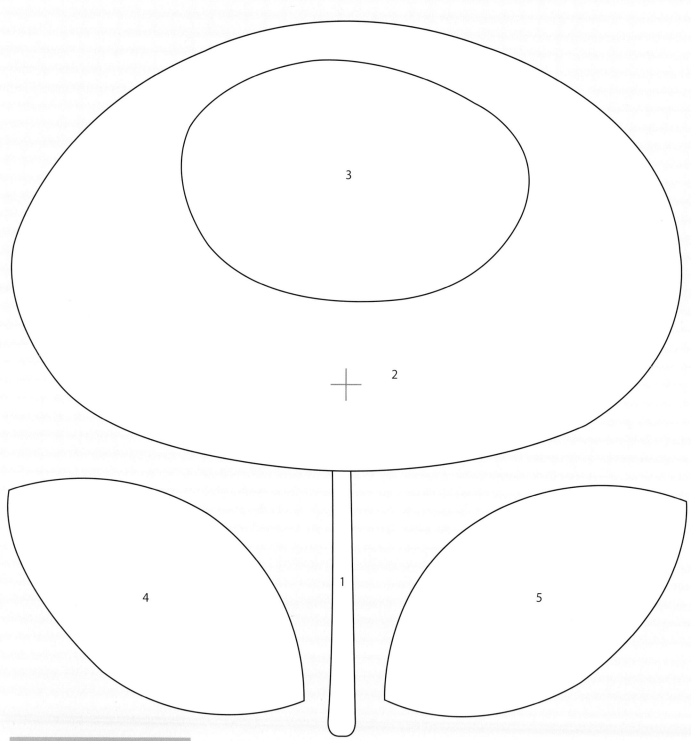

3

2

1

4

5

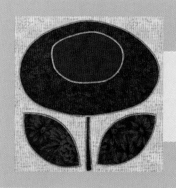

#7 Prairie Princess

2

3

4

1

5

#8 Sundance

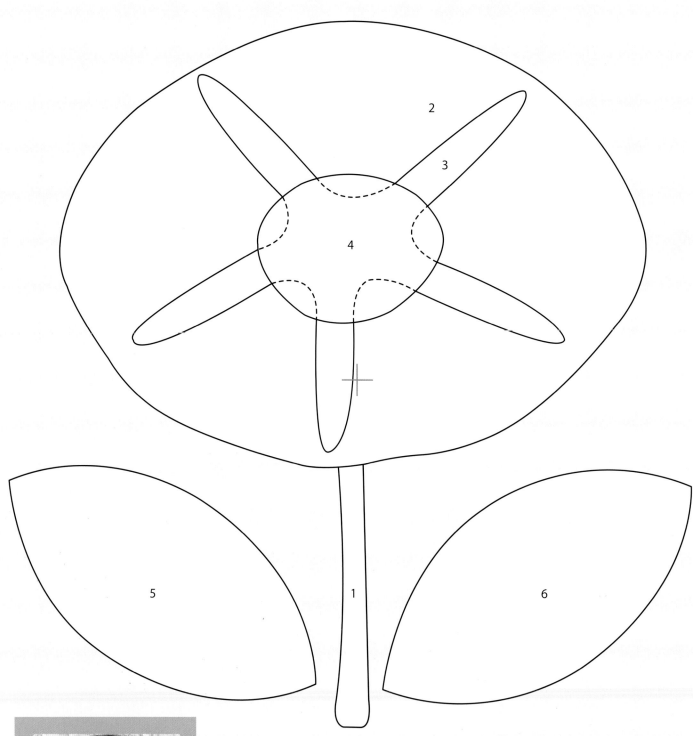

2

3

4

5

1

6

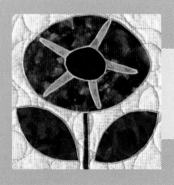

#9 Morning Glory

FLOWER FESTIVAL

#10 Cream Cup

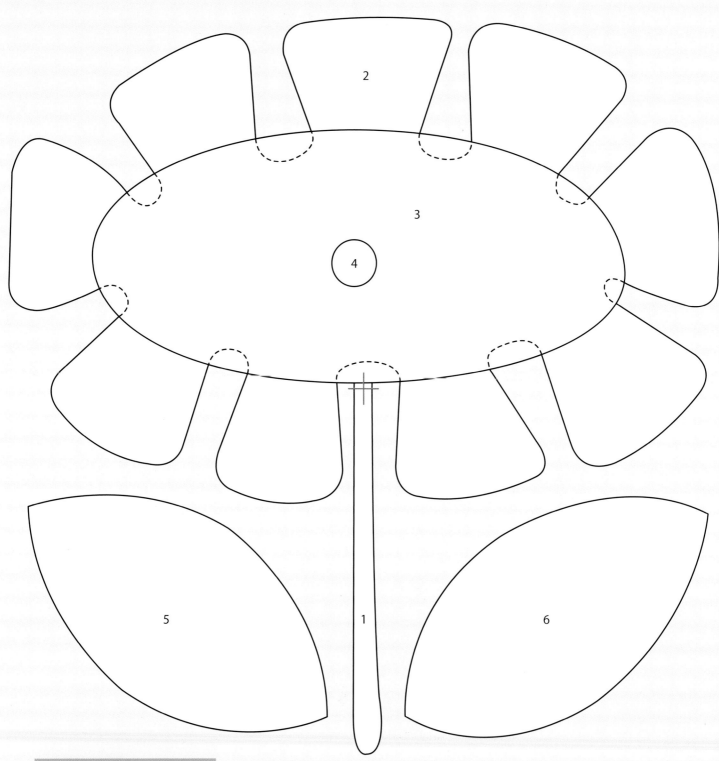

2

3

4

5

1

6

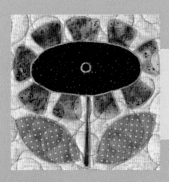

#11 Meadow Clover

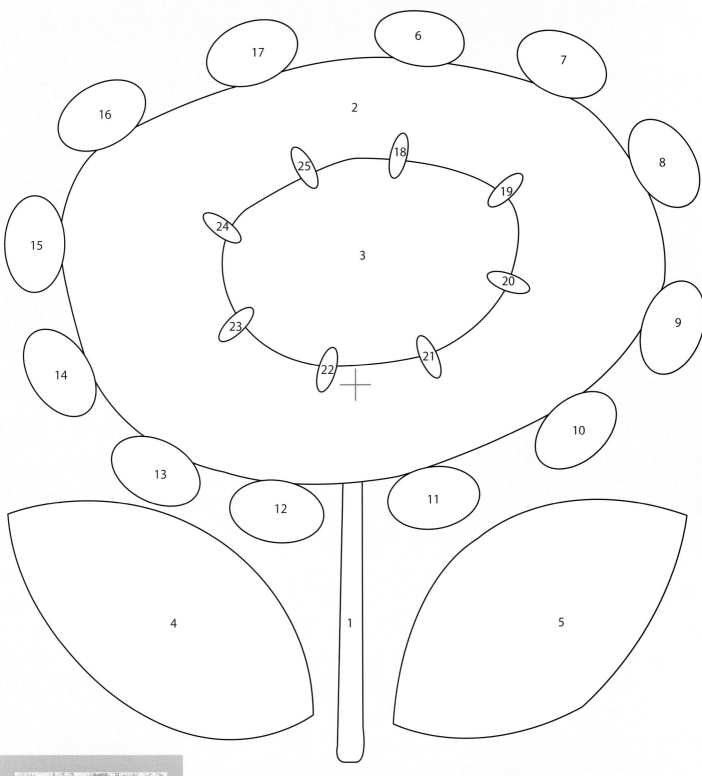

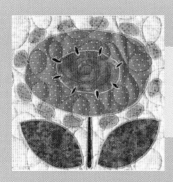

#12 Speckled Bubble

4

5

6

2

1

3

#13 Stardust

FLOWER FESTIVAL

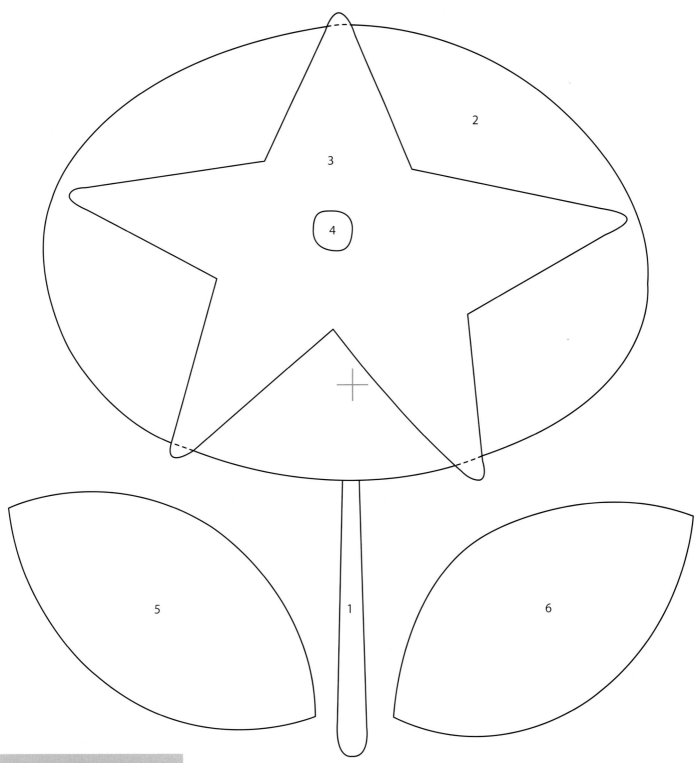

3

2

4

5

1

6

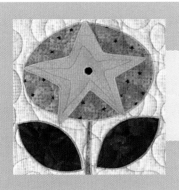

#14 Star Flower

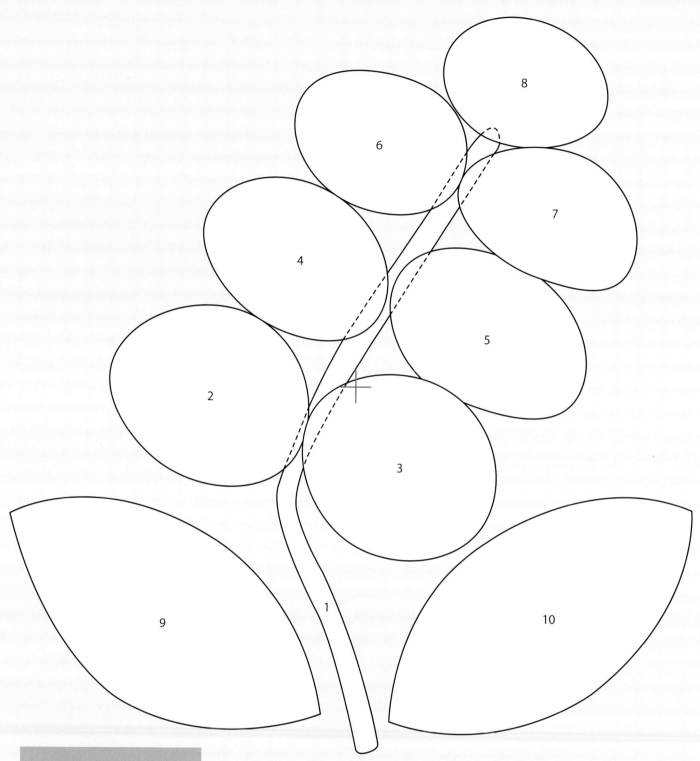

#15 Bunch Berry

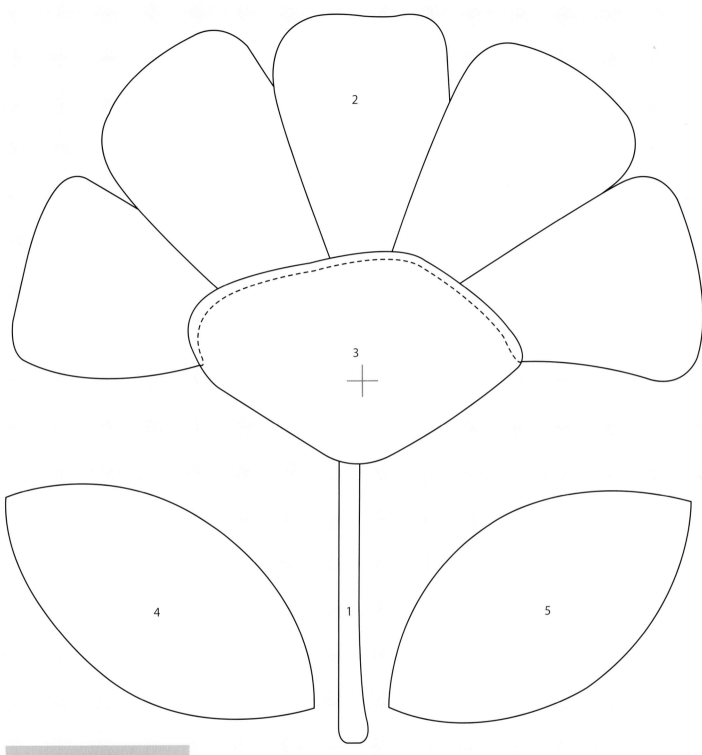

2

3

1

4

5

#16 Buttercup

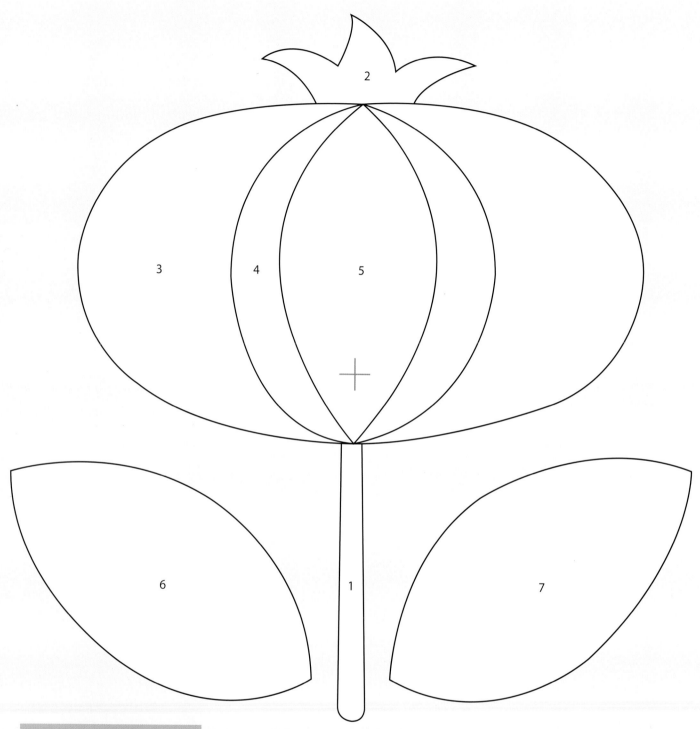

2

3   4   5

6   1   7

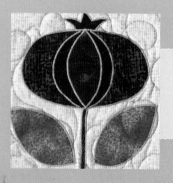

#17 Globe Queen

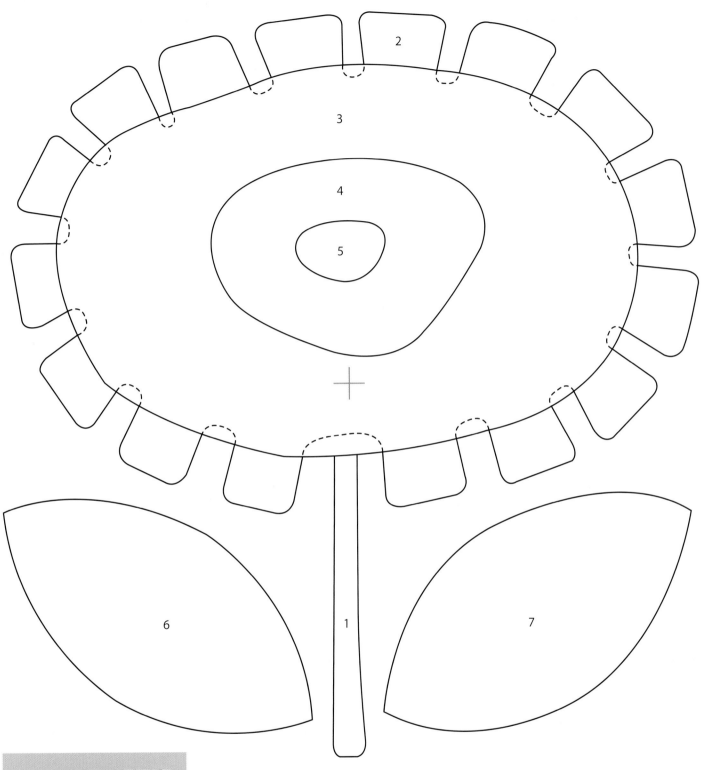

2

3

4

5

6

1

7

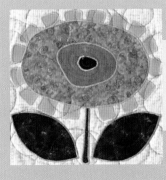

#18 Fringed Happy Flower

4

5

6

2   1   3

#19 Sun Dew

FLOWER FESTIVAL

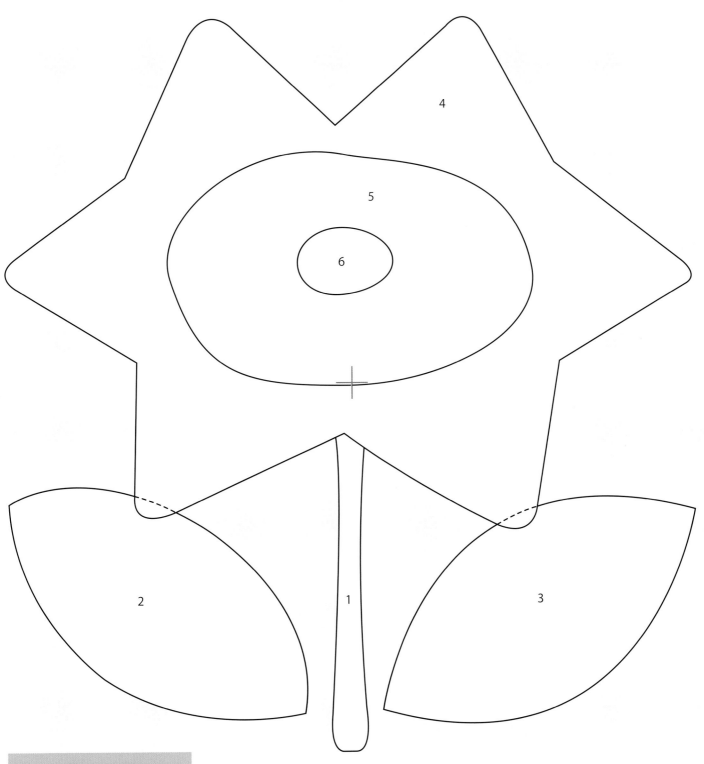

#20 Starburst

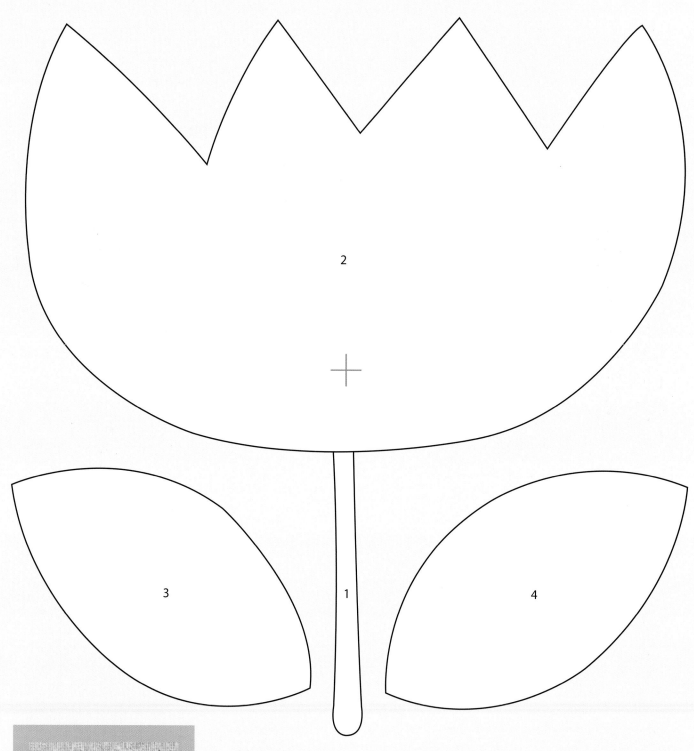

2

3   1   4

#21 Tulip

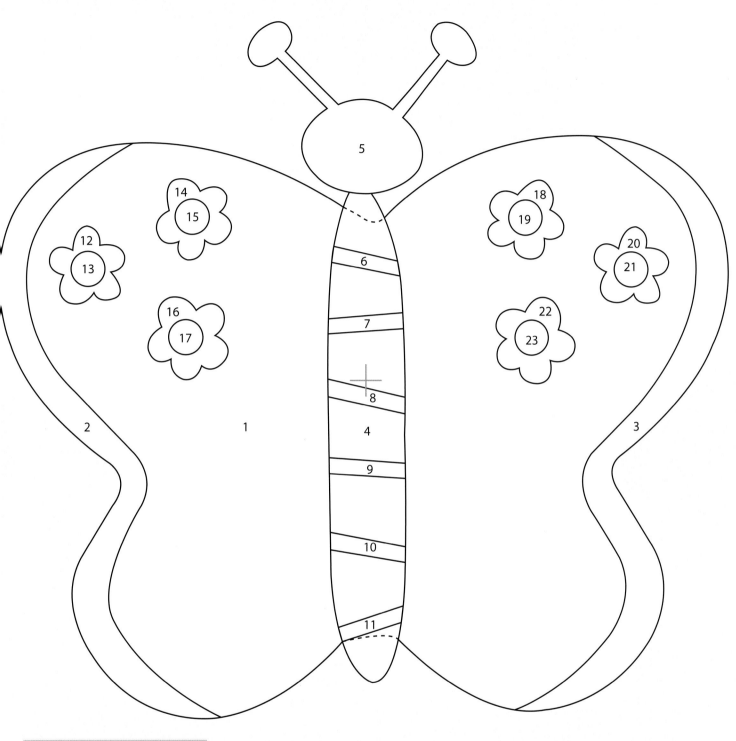

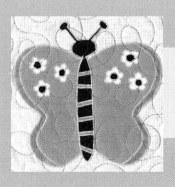

#22 Butterfly

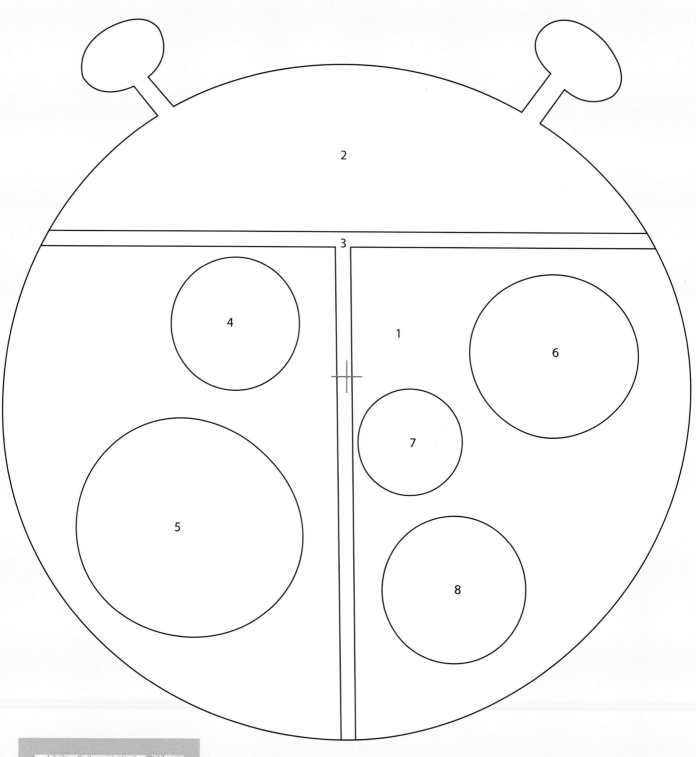

2

3

4

1

6

7

5

8

#23 Ladybug

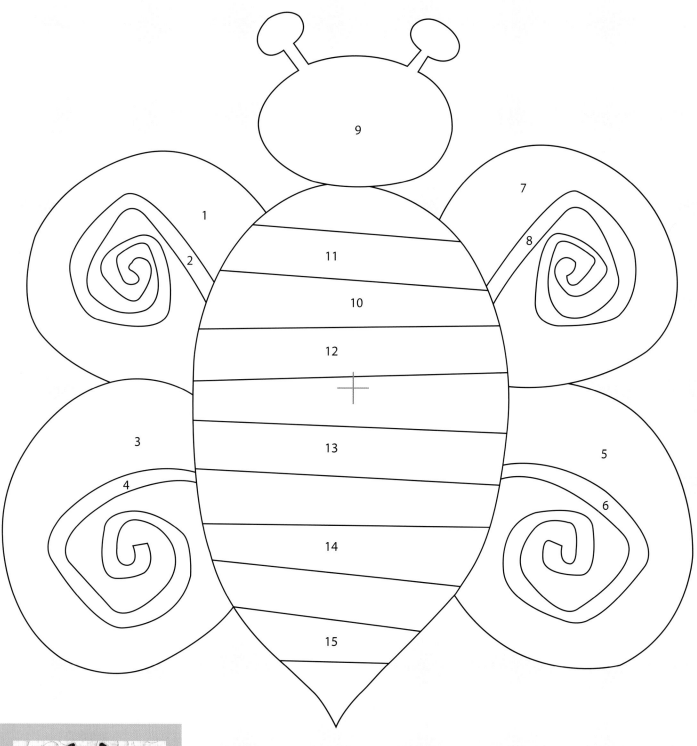

#24 Bumble Bee

v

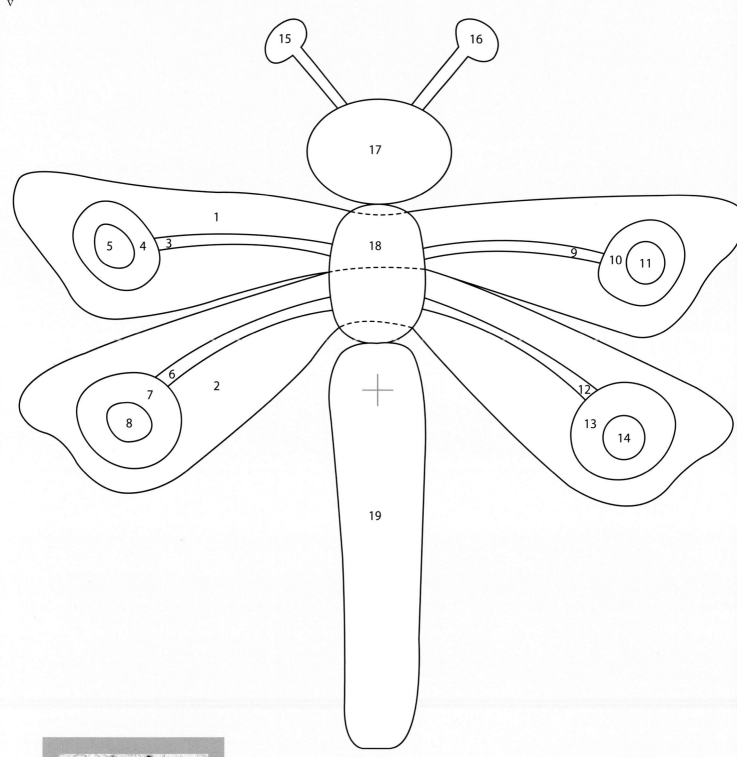

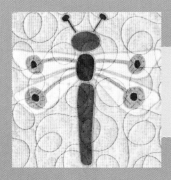

#25 Dragonfly

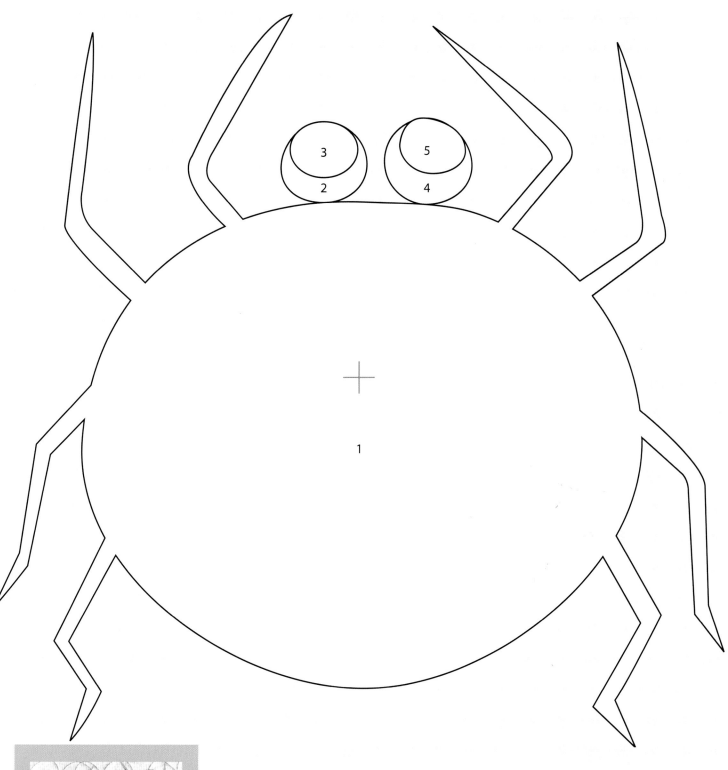

3

5

2

4

1

#26 Spider

#27 Caterpillar

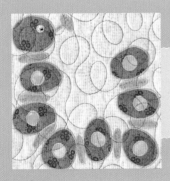

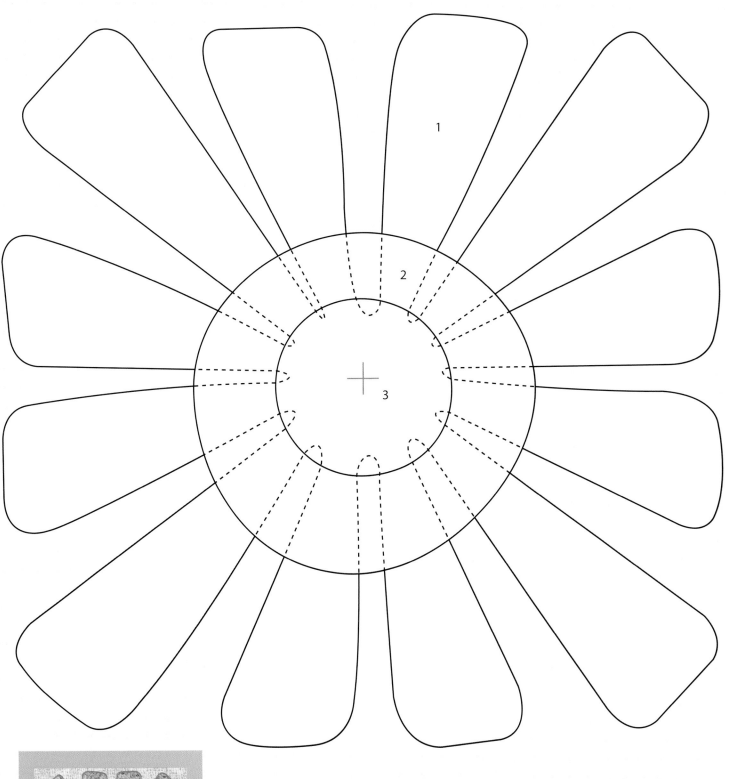

1

2

3

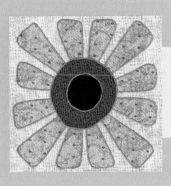

#28 Splatter Flower

1

2

3

#29 Wall Flower

1

2

#30 Tidy Tips

1
2
3

#31 Sparkle Flower

FLOWER FESTIVAL

1

2

3

#32 Swirl Flower

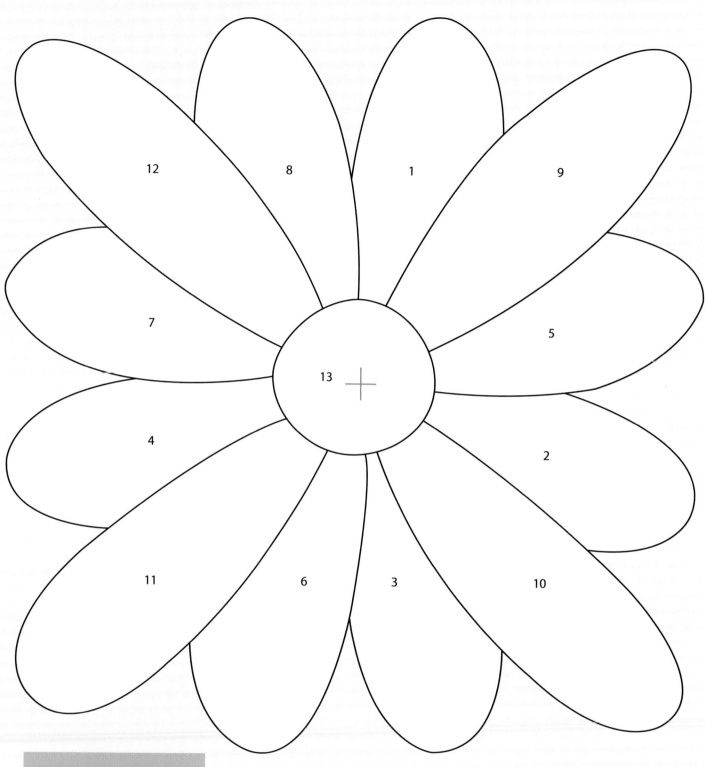

12   8   1   9

7   5

13   +

4   2

11   6   3   10

#33 Aster

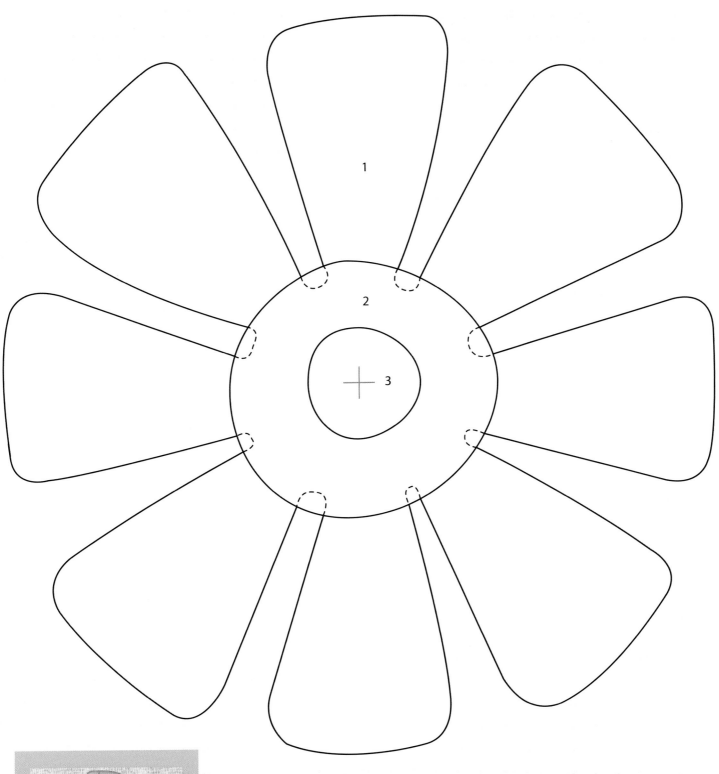

1

2

3

#34 Monkey Flower

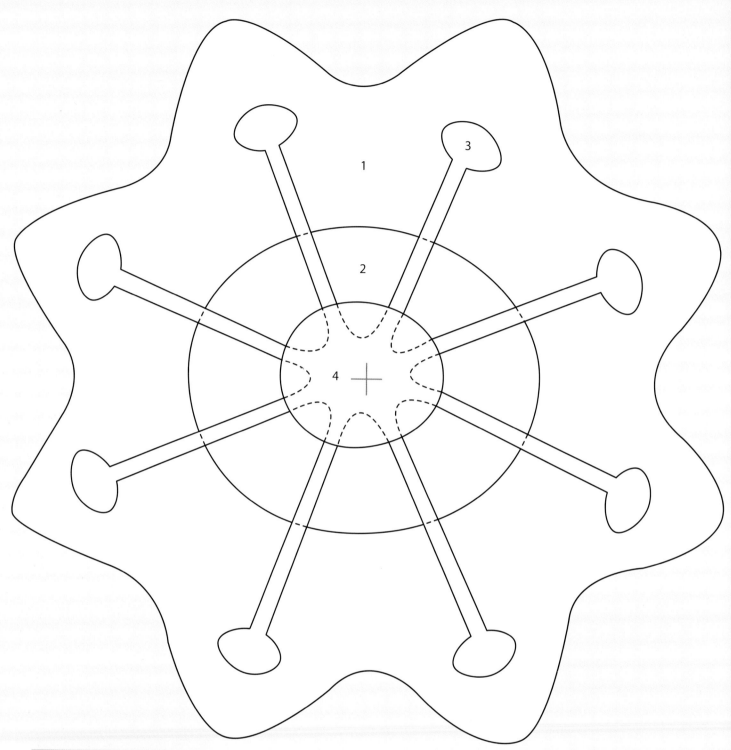

1

3

2

4

#35 Spotted Jewelweed

FLOWER FESTIVAL

1

2

3

4

5

#36 Button Flower

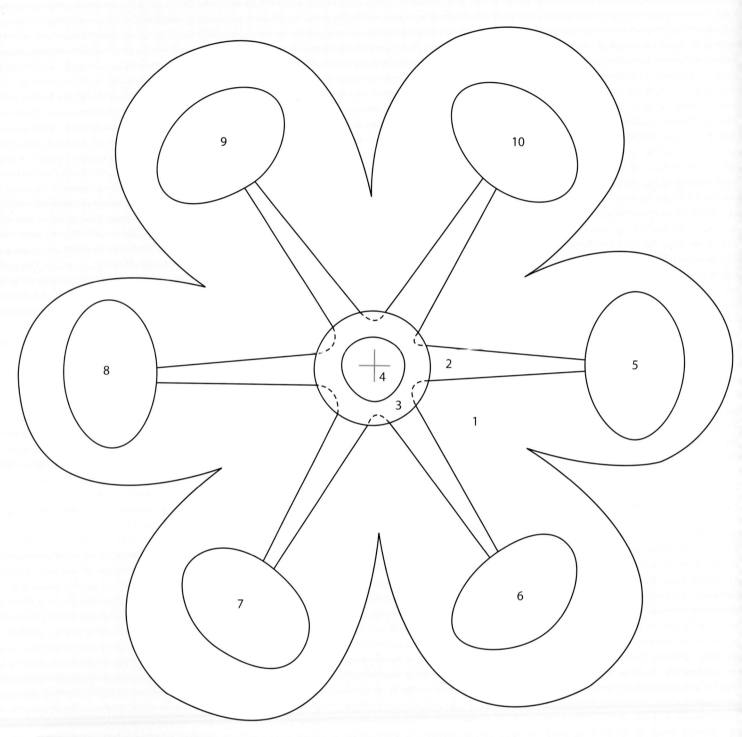

#37 Glory of the Snow

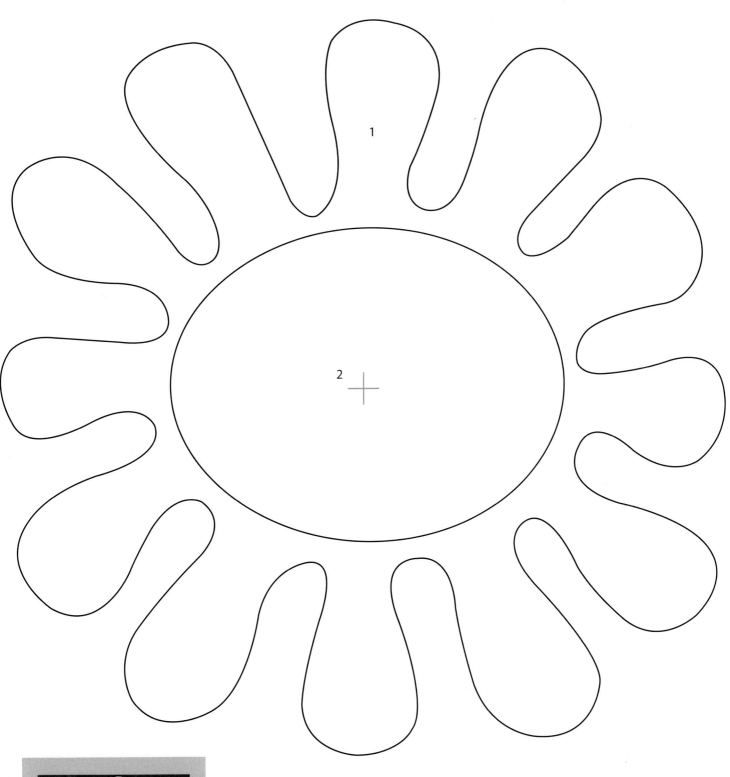

1

2 +

#38 Splash

1

2

#39 Daisy

FLOWER FESTIVAL

1

2

3

4 +

#40 Double Daisy

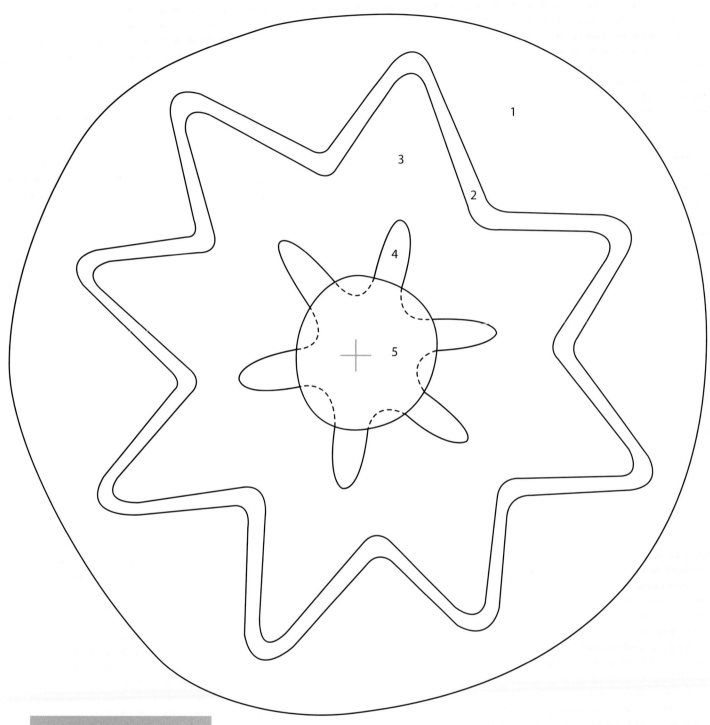

1

3

2

4

5

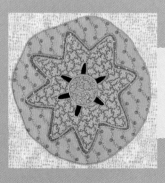

#41 Sand Dollar Flower

#42 Phoebe

6

6

4

4

1

1

5

5

2 3

5

5

1

1

4

4

6

6

#43 Bella

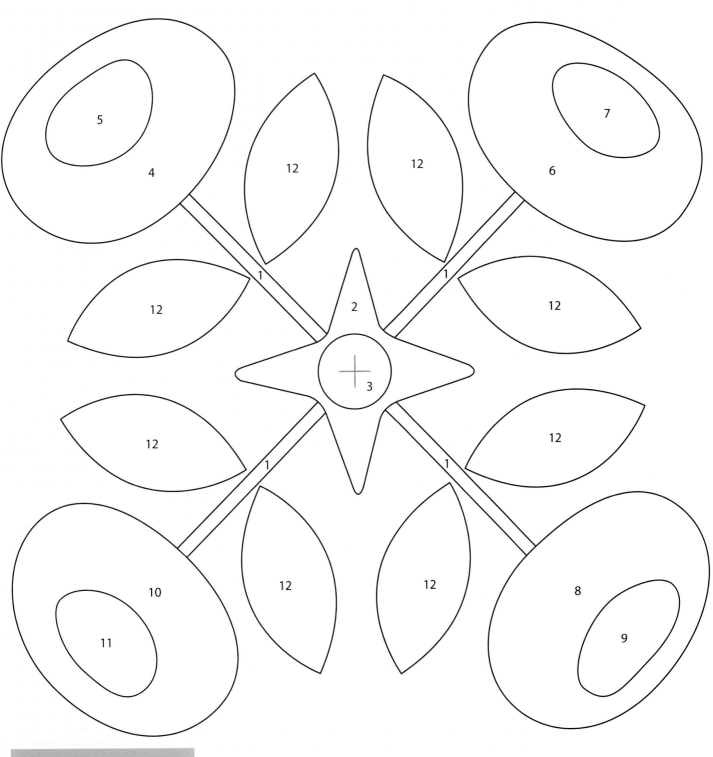

5

4

12

12

7

6

12

1

2

1

12

3

12

1

1

12

10

12

12

8

11

9

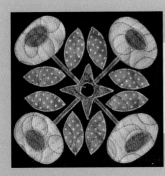

#44 Prairie Princess Cross

#45 Mountain Thistle

FLOWER FESTIVAL

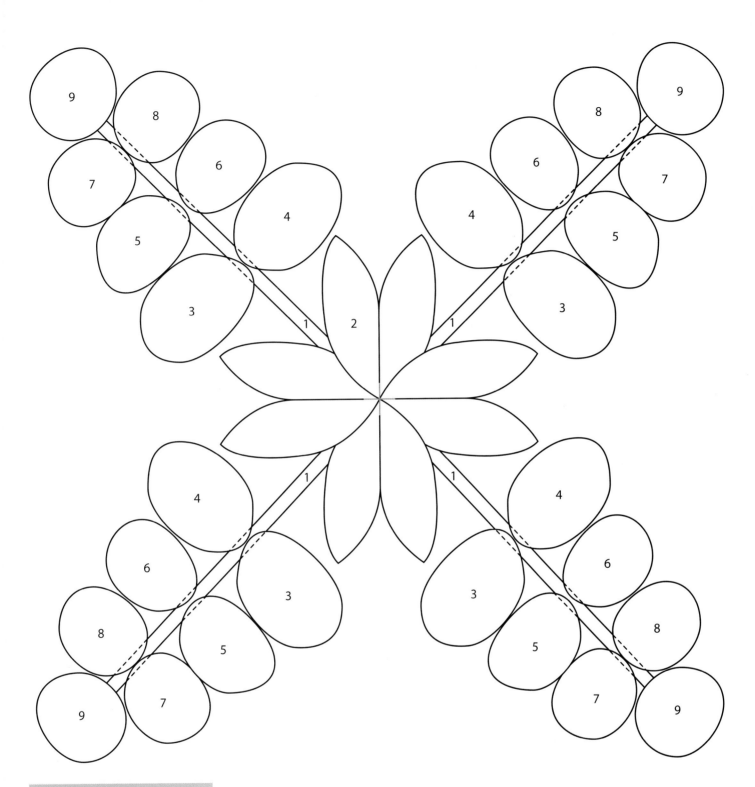

#46 Bunch Berry Bliss

#47 Tulip Twirl

FLOWER FESTIVAL

#48 Star Wreath

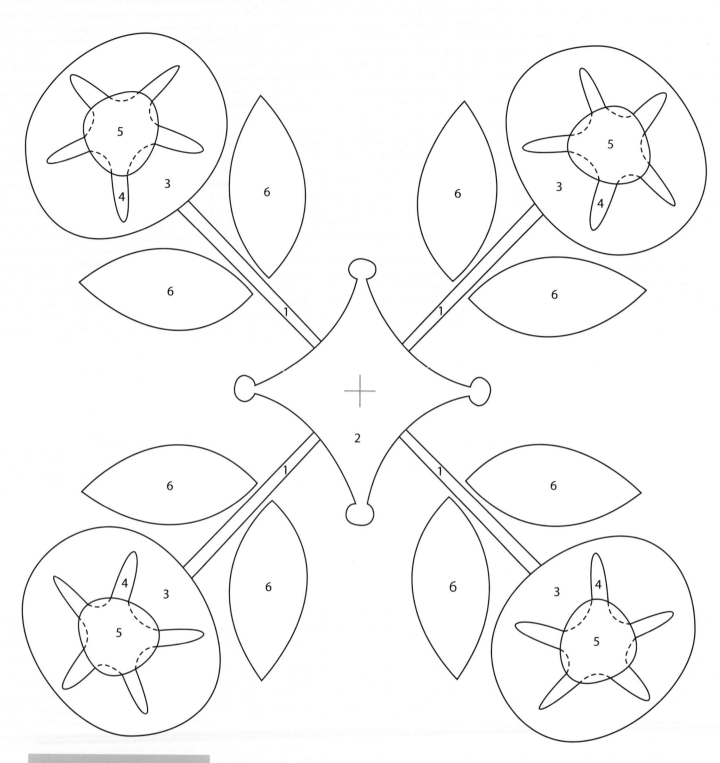

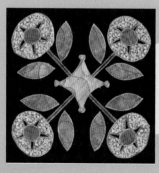

#49 Morning Glory Twirl

#50 Yippee Twist

the Projects

single-block quilts

Finished block size: 8″ × 8″
Finished quilt size: 8½″ × 8½″

Single-block quilts are fast and fun. Select your favorite block (or blocks) and make one, or make a few for a small grouping with a big impact. Framed or unframed, they are sure to add a simple but elegant statement to any room décor. Keep the quilts, or give them away as gifts to someone special.

materials

Materials listed are for 1 single-block quilt.

- ⅓ yard light for appliqué block background
- A variety of scraps for appliqué pieces
- ⅜ yard green for backing and binding
- ¼ yard paper-backed fusible web
- 10″ × 10″ batting

cutting

Cut 1 square 8½″ × 8½″ from the light for the appliqué block background.

appliqué

Refer to Appliqué on page 6.

1. Cut out the appropriate appliqué pieces for your chosen block. Use the patter of your choice from pages 10–59.

2. Appliqué the pieces onto the background.

putting it all together

FINISHING

1. Layer the quilt with batting and backing.

2. Quilt as desired, and bind.

3. Hang the quilt as it is, or mat and frame it as desired.

pinwheel *table runner*

Quilted by Julie Karasek of Patched Works, Inc.

Brighten your table with this cheerful pinwheel table runner in the classic color combination of red and white.

Finished block size: 8″ × 8″

Finished table runner size: 23″ × 57″

 materials

- 1 yard total assorted lights for appliqué block backgrounds and pinwheel blocks
- 1¼ yards total assorted reds for pinwheel blocks and appliqué pieces
- 2 yards for backing and binding
- ¾ yard paper-backed fusible web
- 26″ × 61″ batting

 cutting

Cut 5 squares 8½″ × 8½″ from the assorted lights for the appliqué block backgrounds.

Cut 16 squares 4⅞″ × 4⅞″ from the assorted lights for the pinwheel blocks. Cut the squares once diagonally for a total of 32 triangles.

Cut 16 squares 4⅞″ × 4⅞″ from the assorted reds for the pinwheel blocks. Cut the squares once diagonally for a total of 32 triangles.

Cut squares once diagonally.

 appliqué

Refer to Appliqué on page 6.

1. Cut out 5 each of appliqué pieces 1, 2, and 3 (the pattern is on page 37).

2. Appliqué the appropriate pieces onto each background.

pinwheel blocks

1. Sew a light triangle to a red triangle on the diagonal edges. Make 32 triangle squares. Press toward the red triangles.

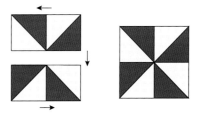

Sew triangles; make 32.

2. Piece the pinwheel blocks. Press. Make 8.

Piece pinwheel blocks; make 8.

putting it all together

Arrange and sew the pinwheel blocks and the flower blocks into rows as shown. Press. Sew together the rows. Press.

FINISHING

1. Layer the table runner with batting and backing, and baste or pin.

2. Quilt as desired, and bind.

Putting it all together

log cabin *table topper*

Quilted by Julie Karasek of Patched Works, Inc.

Finished block size: 8″ × 8″
Finished table topper size: 48½″ × 48½″

The Log Cabin block is a well-loved favorite among quilters. Here the Log Cabin blocks are framed by a fun, fresh appliquéd flower block border. This luminous quilt will brighten any tabletop but would also look great as a wall quilt.

❋ materials

- 2¼ yards total assorted dark and medium greens for Log Cabin blocks and appliqué block backgrounds
- 1 yard total assorted light greens for Log Cabin blocks
- 2 yards total assorted reds, yellows, oranges, and pinks for appliquéd flowers
- 3⅜ yards for backing and binding
- 4½ yards paper-backed fusible web
- 52″ × 52″ batting

❋ cutting

Cut 20 squares 8½″ × 8½″ from the assorted dark and medium greens for the appliqué block backgrounds.

Cut the following from the assorted dark and medium greens for the Log Cabin blocks:

    16 squares 2½″ × 2½″

    16 rectangles 1½″ × 3½″

    16 rectangles 1½″ × 4½″

    16 rectangles 1½″ × 5½″

    16 rectangles 1½″ × 6½″

    16 rectangles 1½″ × 7½″

    16 rectangles 1½″ × 8½″

Cut the following from the assorted light greens for the Log Cabin blocks:

    16 rectangles 1½″ × 2½″

    16 rectangles 1½″ × 3½″

    16 rectangles 1½″ × 4½″

    16 rectangles 1½″ × 5½″

    16 rectangles 1½″ × 6½″

    16 rectangles 1½″ × 7½″

❋ appliqué

Refer to Appliqué on page 6.

1. Cut out 20 each of appliqué pieces 1, 2, 3, and 4 (the pattern is on page 49).

2. Appliqué the appropriate pieces onto each background.

❋ log cabin blocks

Piece the Log Cabin blocks by adding the logs one at a time in a clockwise direction as shown. Press after each addition. Make 16 blocks.

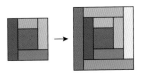

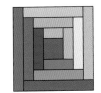

Make 16.

❋ putting it all together

BLOCKS

1. Arrange and sew together 4 rows of 4 Log Cabin blocks. Press.

2. Sew together the rows to make the pieced block section of the table topper. Press.

APPLIQUÉD BORDER

1. Arrange and sew together 2 rows of 4 appliqué blocks to make the side borders. Press. Sew the side borders to the table topper. Press toward the borders.

2. Arrange and sew together 2 rows of 6 appliqué blocks to make the top and bottom borders. Press. Sew the top and bottom borders to the table topper. Press toward the borders.

FINISHING

1. Layer the table topper with batting and backing, and baste or pin.

2. Quilt as desired, and bind.

Putting it all together

bug brigade *wall quilt*

Quilted by Lynn Helmke

Finished block size: 12″ × 12″
Finished wall quilt size: 32½″ × 44½″

Fun and friendly bugs are the focus of this wall quilt. Fabulous for a child or any bug lover, these blocks would make great single-block quilts as well.

 ## materials

- ⅝ yard light for appliqué block backgrounds
- ¾ yard total assorted scraps for appliquéd bugs
- ¾ yard total assorted greens for appliqué block borders
- ⅔ yard black for border
- 1⅞ yards for backing and binding
- 1½ yards paper-backed fusible web
- 36″ × 48″ batting

cutting

Cut 6 squares 8½″ × 8½″ from the light for the appliqué block backgrounds.

Cut the following from the assorted greens for the appliqué block borders:

> 12 strips 1½″ × 8½″
> 24 strips 1½″ × 10½″
> 12 strips 1½″ × 12½″

Cut the following from the black for the outer borders:

> 2 strips 4½″ × 36½″ for the 2 side outer borders
> 2 strips 4½″ × 32½″ for the top and bottom outer borders

appliqué

Refer to Appliqué on page 6.

1. Cut out the appliqué pieces for each bug (the patterns are on pages 31–36).

2. Appliqué the appropriate pieces onto each background.

APPLIQUÉ BLOCK BORDERS

1. Sew a 1½″ × 8½″ strip to the top and bottom of each block. Press toward the strips.

2. Sew a 1½″ × 10½″ strip to the sides of each block. Press toward the strips.

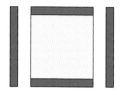

Add border strips to blocks.

3. Sew a 1½″ × 10½″ strip to the top and bottom of each block. Press toward the outer strips.

4. Sew a 1½″ × 12½″ strip to the sides of each block. Press toward the outer strips.

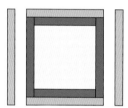

Add remaining border strips to blocks.

 ## putting it all together

BLOCKS

Arrange and sew together 3 rows of 2 blocks. Press. Sew together the rows. Press.

BORDER

1. Sew the side outer borders to the quilt top, and press toward the borders.

2. Sew the top and bottom outer borders to the quilt top, and press toward the borders.

FINISHING

1. Layer the quilt with batting and backing, and baste or pin.

2. Quilt as desired, and bind.

Putting it all together

antique flower garden *wall quilt*

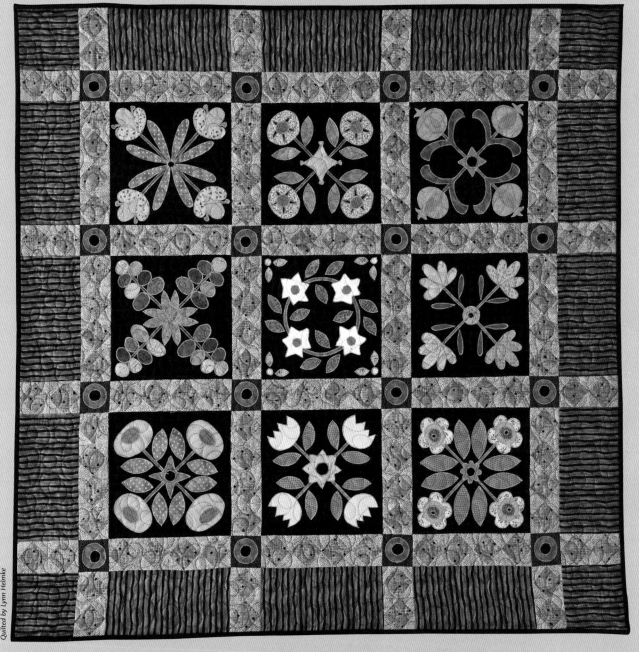

Quilted by Lynn Helmke

Finished block size: 8″ × 8″

Finished wall quilt size: 40½″ × 40½″

Recapture images of gardens past with this wall quilt. Soft sage foliage and pastel flowers give this quilt an old-fashioned charm.

ANTIQUE FLOWER GARDEN WALL QUILT   71

❀ materials

- 1¼ yards black for appliqué block backgrounds, small appliquéd flower center circles, and small appliquéd lattice circles
- ½ yard total assorted greens for stems and leaves
- ¾ yard total assorted blues, yellows, pinks, purples, oranges, and light cream for appliquéd flowers
- ¾ yard dark tan for square-in-a-square lattice
- 1 yard tan for square-in-a-square lattice
- ¼ yard dark brown for lattice connecting squares
- ⅛ yard brown for large appliquéd circles
- ¾ yard brown and black stripe for outer pieced border
- 2¾ yards for backing and binding
- 2¾ yards paper-backed fusible web
- 44″ × 44″ batting

❀ cutting

Cut 9 squares 8½″ × 8½″ from the black for the appliqué block backgrounds.

Cut 128 squares 2½″ × 2½″ from the dark tan for the square-in-a-square lattice.

Cut 512 squares 1½″ × 1½″ from the tan for the square-in-a-square lattice.

Cut 16 squares 2½″ × 2½″ from the dark brown for the lattice connecting squares.

Cut 12 rectangles 8½″ × 4½″ from the brown and black stripe for the outer pieced border.

Cut 4 squares 4½″ × 4½″ from the brown and black stripe for the outer pieced border.

❀ appliqué

Refer to Appliqué on page 6.

1. Cut out the appliqué pieces for the flowers, stems, and leaves (the patterns are on pages 51–59).

2. Appliqué the appropriate pieces onto each background.

3. Cut out 16 each of circle pattern pieces 1 and 2 for the lattice connecting squares (the patterns are on page 74).

4. Appliqué the circle pieces onto each square.

Appliqué lattice connecting squares.

square-in-a-square lattice

1. Draw a diagonal line from corner to corner on the wrong side of each of the 1½" tan squares.

2. With right sides together, layer a 1½" tan square on 2 opposite corners of a 2½" dark tan square. Sew together the squares on the drawn lines. Trim to ¼" from the seamline, and press open.

Stitch, trim, and press.

3. Repeat Step 2 for the remaining 2 corners of the dark tan square. Press open. Make 128 blocks.

Stitch, trim, and press.

Make 128 blocks.

putting it all together

1. Sew together 24 strips of 4 square-in-a-square lattice blocks. Press.

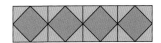

Piece long lattice strips; make 24.

2. Sew together 16 strips of 2 square-in-a-square lattice blocks each. Press.

Piece short lattice strips; make 16.

3. Alternate 4 of the 4-square lattice strips with 3 appliqué blocks, and sew together the strips and blocks to make an appliqué block row. Press. Make 3 rows.

4. Sew an 8½" × 4½" brown and black stripe rectangle to each end of the appliqué block rows. Press.

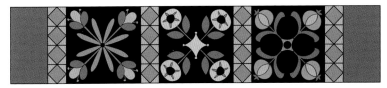

Sew appliqué block row; make 3.

5. Sew together the horizontal lattice strips as shown. Press. Make 4.

Sew horizontal lattice strips; make 4.

6. Sew the appliqué block rows between the horizontal lattice strips. Press.

7. Alternate the 2-square lattice strips with 3 brown and black stripe rectangles 8½" × 4½", and sew together the strips and blocks. Sew a 4½" × 4½" brown and black stripe square to each end to make the top and bottom borders as shown. Press.

Sew top and bottom borders.

8. Sew the top and bottom borders to the quilt top. Press.

FINISHING

1. Layer the quilt with batting and backing, and baste or pin.

2. Quilt as desired, and bind.

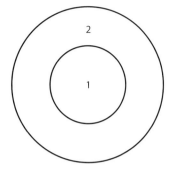

Lattice connecting square appliqué circle patterns

Putting it all together

bloomin' beauties
wall quilt

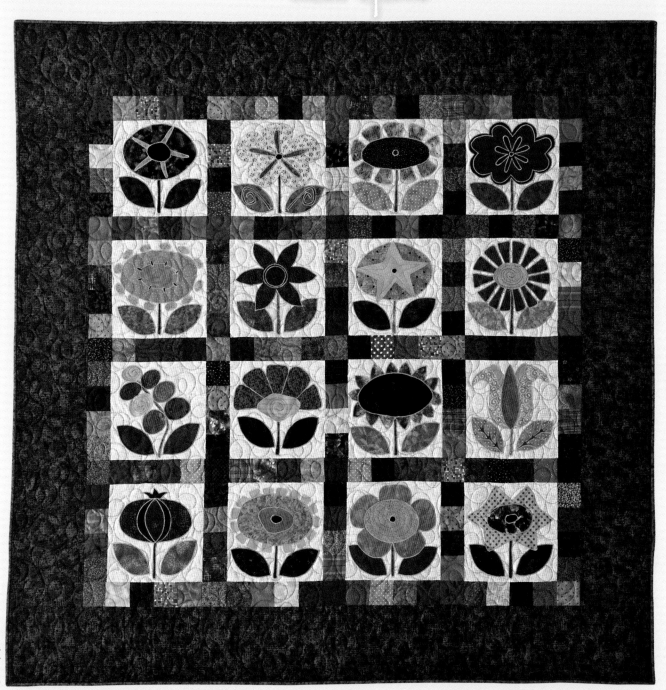

Quilted by Lynn Helmke

Finished block size: 8″ × 8″
Finished wall quilt size: 54½″ × 54½″

Pick 16 different blocks to make this happy wall quilt bursting with plump, cheery blossoms.

 materials

- 1¼ yards light for appliqué block backgrounds

- 1½ yards total assorted golds, pinks, blues, purples, reds, and oranges for appliquéd flowers

- Scraps of black for flower centers

- 1½ yards total assorted greens for pieced lattice and appliquéd stems and leaves

- 1⅝ yards dark green for border (cut lengthwise on the fabric)

  You will need 1⅓ yards if you choose to cut the borders crosswise and piece them.

- 3¾ yards for backing and binding

- 4 yards paper-backed fusible web

- 59″ × 59″ batting

 appliqué

Refer to Appliqué on page 6.

1. Cut out the appropriate appliqué pieces for your chosen blocks. The patterns are found on pages 10–59.

2. Appliqué the appropriate pieces onto each background.

 putting it all together

1. Arrange and sew together 20 strips of 4 squares 2½″ × 2½″ from the assorted greens to make the vertical lattice strips. Press.

Piece vertical lattice strips; make 20.

2. Arrange and sew together 5 strips of 21 squares 2½″ × 2½″ from the assorted greens to make the horizontal lattice strips. Press.

Piece horizontal lattice strips; make 5.

3. Alternate 5 vertical lattice strips with 4 appliqué blocks, and sew together the blocks and strips to make an appliqué block row. Press. Make 4 appliqué block rows.

4. Sew the appliqué block rows between the horizontal lattice strips. Press.

BORDER

1. Sew the side borders to the quilt top, and press toward the borders.

2. Sew the top and bottom borders to the quilt top, and press toward the borders.

Putting it all together

cutting

Cut 16 squares 8½″ × 8½″ from the light for the appliqué block backgrounds.

Cut 185 squares 2½″ × 2½″ from the assorted greens for the pieced lattice.

Cut the following lengthwise strips from the dark green*:

2 strips 6½″ × 42½″ for the side borders

2 strips 6½″ × 54½″ for the top and bottom borders

If cutting crosswise, cut 6 strips 6½″ × fabric width, piece the strips end to end as necessary, and cut the borders.

FINISHING

1. Layer the quilt with batting and backing, and baste or pin.

2. Quilt as desired, and bind.

splash lap quilt

Quilted by Julie Karasek of Patched Works, Inc.

Finished block size: 8″ × 8″

Finished lap quilt size: 60½″ × 76½″

This quilt is easier than it looks! The quilt body is made up of simple appliquéd squares with rounded corners—no awkward stopping and starting. Both block designs allow continuous line appliqué. Highly contrasting colors in rich tones give this quilt a contemporary twist.

materials

- 1¾ yards total assorted olive greens for appliqué block backgrounds and appliqué pieces

- 1¾ yards total assorted browns for appliqué block backgrounds and appliqué pieces

- 1¾ yards total assorted teals for appliqué block backgrounds and appliqué pieces

- 1¾ yards total assorted deep reds for appliqué block backgrounds and appliqué pieces

- ⅞ yard total assorted tans for appliqué block backgrounds and appliqué pieces

- ⅔ yard tan for inner border

- 5¼ yards for backing and binding

- 6½ yards paper-backed fusible web

- 64″ × 80″ batting

cutting

Cut the following from the assorted olive greens:
  14 squares 8½″ × 8½″ for the appliquéd flower block backgrounds

  7 squares 8½″ × 8½″ for the appliquéd square blocks

Cut the following from the assorted browns:
  14 squares 8½″ × 8½″ for the appliquéd flower block backgrounds

  7 squares 8½″ × 8½″ for the appliquéd square blocks

Cut 7 squares 8½″ × 8½″ from the assorted teals for the appliquéd square blocks.

Cut 7 squares 8½″ × 8½″ from the assorted deep reds for the appliquéd square blocks.

Cut 7 squares 8½″ × 8½″ from the assorted tans for the appliquéd square blocks.

Cut 8 strips 2½″ × fabric width from the tan for the inner borders. Piece the strips end to end as necessary, and cut the following:

  2 strips 2½″ × 56½″ for the 2 side inner borders

  2 strips 2½″ × 60½″ for the top and bottom inner borders

  4 strips 2½″ × 8½″

appliqué

Refer to Appliqué on page 6.

1. Cut out 28 each of flower appliqué pieces 1 and 2 (the pattern is on page 47). Cut out 35 each of square appliqué pieces 3 and 4 (the pattern is on page 80).

2. Appliqué the appropriate pieces onto each background. Make 28 flower blocks and 35 square blocks.

Appliquéd square blocks; make 35.

putting it all together

APPLIQUÉD SQUARE BLOCKS

1. Arrange and sew together 7 rows of 5 blocks. Press.

2. Sew together the rows. Press.

SIDE BORDERS

1. Sew the tan inner side borders 2½″ × 56½″ to the quilt top. Press toward the borders.

2. Arrange and sew together 2 rows of 7 flower blocks to make the outer side borders. Press.

3. Sew the outer borders to the quilt top. Press toward the inner borders.

TOP AND BOTTOM BORDERS

1. Sew the tan inner top and bottom borders 2½" × 60½" to the quilt top. Press toward the borders.

2. Arrange and sew together 2 rows of 5 flower blocks to make the outer top and bottom borders. Press.

3. Sew a tan strip 2½" × 8½" to each end of the flower block rows. Press toward the tan strip.

4. Sew a flower block to each end of the rows to complete the outer top and bottom borders. Press toward the tan strip. Sew the outer borders to the quilt top. Press toward the inner borders.

FINISHING

1. Layer the quilt with batting and backing, and baste or pin.

2. Quilt as desired, and bind.

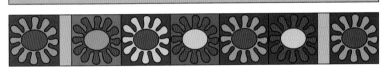

Putting it all together

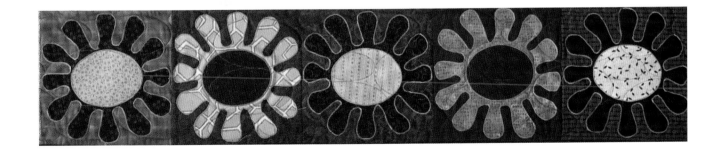

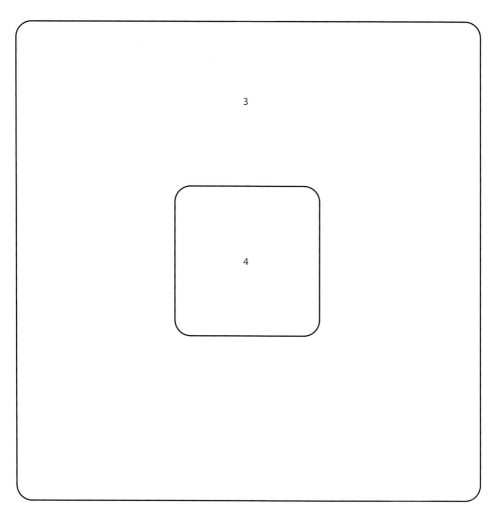

Square block appliqué pieces

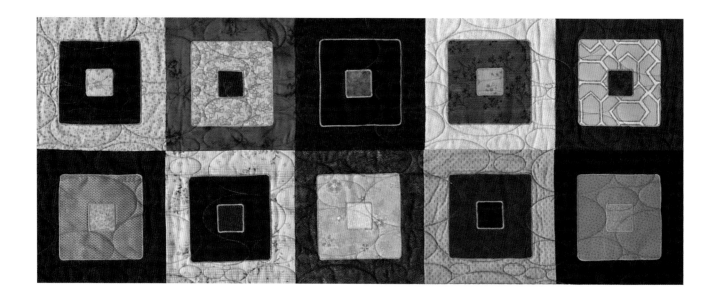

FLOWER FESTIVAL

tulip lap quilt

Quilted by Lynn Helmke

Finished block size: 12″ × 12″

Finished lap quilt size: 76½″ × 88½″

Springtime means tulips. Keep the memory of tulips and spring alive throughout the year with this stunning but simple quilt. The rich combination of purple, green, and black makes this quilt radiant.

 materials

- 2⅛ yards black for appliqué block backgrounds
- 1 yard total assorted purples for tulips
- 3¾ yards total assorted greens for appliqué block borders and appliquéd stems and leaves
- ⅔ yard green for inner border
- 2¼ yards black for appliquéd outer border (cut lengthwise)

  You will need 1⅔ yards if you choose to cut the borders crosswise and piece them.

- 5¾ yards backing and binding
- 4 yards paper-backed fusible web
- 80″ × 92″ batting

 cutting

Cut 30 squares 8½″ × 8½″ from the black for the appliqué block backgrounds.

Cut the following from the assorted greens for the appliqué block borders:

> 30 strips 2½″ × 8½″
>
> 60 strips 2½″ × 10½″
>
> 30 strips 2½″ × 12½″

Cut 8 strips 2½″ × fabric width from the green for the inner border. Piece the strips end to end as necessary, and cut the following:

> 2 strips 2½″ × 72½″ for the side inner borders
>
> 2 strips 2½″ × 64½″ for the top and bottom inner borders

Cut 4 lengthwise strips 6½″ × 76½″ from the black for the appliquéd outer border.*

*If cutting crosswise, cut 9 strips 6½″ × fabric width, piece the strips end to end as necessary, and cut the borders.

 appliqué

Refer to Appliqué on page 6.

1. Cut out 30 each of appliqué pieces 1, 2, 3, and 4 (the pattern is on page 30).

2. Appliqué the appropriate pieces onto each background.

APPLIQUÉ BORDERS

Follow the border sequence numbers, and sew the border strips to the appliqué blocks. Press toward the border strip after each addition.

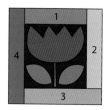

Piece blocks; make 30.

 putting it all together

Arrange and sew together 6 rows of 5 blocks. Press. Sew together the rows. Press.

INNER BORDER

1. Sew the side inner borders to the quilt top. Press toward the borders.

2. Sew the top and bottom inner borders to the quilt top. Press toward the borders.

APPLIQUÉD BORDER

1. Sew the side appliquéd borders to the quilt top. Press toward the inner borders. Sew the top and bottom appliquéd borders to the quilt top. Press toward the inner borders.

2. Cut out 36 of appliqué piece 4. Cut out 4 of appliqué piece 5 (the patterns are on pages 30 and 83).

3. Appliqué the appropriate pieces onto the border.

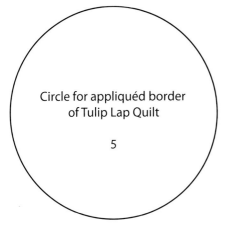

Circle for appliquéd border
of Tulip Lap Quilt

5

FINISHING

1. Layer the quilt with batting and backing, and baste or pin.

2. Quilt as desired, and bind.

Putting it all together

daisy days *lap quilt*

Quilted by Julie Karasek of Patched Works, Inc.

Finished block size: 8″ × 8″
Finished lap quilt size: 72½″ × 88½″

Scrappy pieced block borders frame black-eyed daisies in warm, vibrant colors. Tan appliqué block backgrounds give this quilt its folk art charm.

# materials

- 3⅛ yards total assorted tans for appliqué block backgrounds
- 1⅜ yards total assorted blacks for flower centers and inner border
- 5 yards total assorted reds, purples, blues, oranges, pinks, and yellows for appliquéd flowers and outer pieced border
- 6 yards for backing and binding
- 5 yards of paper-backed fusible web
- 76″ × 92″ batting

cutting

Cut 48 squares 8½″ × 8½″ from the assorted tans for the appliqué block backgrounds.

Cut 240 squares 2½″ × 2½″ from the assorted blacks for the inner pieced borders.

Cut 36 squares 8½″ × 8½″ from the assorted reds, purples, blues, oranges, pinks, and yellows for the outer pieced borders.

# appliqué

Refer to Appliqué on page 6.

1. Cut out 48 each of appliqué pieces 1 and 2 (the pattern is on page 48).

2. Appliqué the appropriate pieces onto each background.

putting it all together

BLOCKS

Arrange and sew together 8 rows of 6 blocks. Press. Sew together the rows. Press.

INNER PIECED BORDER

1. Arrange and sew together 4 rows of 32 squares 2½″ × 2½″ from the assorted blacks to make the side inner pieced borders. Press. Sew together the rows in pairs. Press.

2. Sew the side inner pieced borders to the quilt top. Press.

3. Sew together 4 rows of 28 squares 2½″ × 2½″ from the assorted blacks to make the top and bottom inner pieced borders. Press. Sew together the rows in pairs. Press.

4. Sew the top and bottom inner pieced borders to the quilt top. Press.

OUTER PIECED BORDER

1. Arrange and sew together 4 rows of 9 squares 8½″ × 8½″ from the assorted reds, purples, blues, oranges, pinks, and yellows. Press.

2. Sew the side outer pieced borders to the quilt top. Press.

3. Sew the top and bottom outer pieced borders to the quilt top. Press.

FINISHING

1. Layer the quilt with batting and backing, and baste or pin.

2. Quilt as desired, and bind.

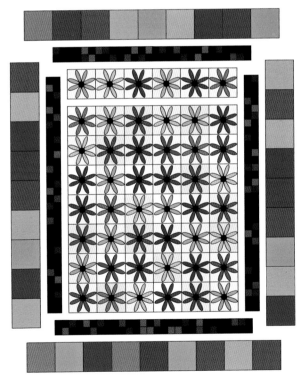

Putting it all together

about the author

At age 23, Kim took her first quilting class and was immediately hooked. She began designing professionally in 1996, when her pattern company, Little Quilt Company, made its debut at the Quilt Market in Minneapolis. In addition to designing quilt patterns, Kim designs fabric for Andover/ Makower and works with Leo Licensing, which licenses her designs for nonfabric products. Kim has authored several books with C&T Publishing.

Kim is from southeastern Wisconsin, where she lives with her husband, Gary; her sons Ben, Sam, and Gator; and her dog, Rio. Her son Max attends college in Minnesota; her daughter Cody lives nearby, and her daughter Ali lives in Portland. Kim's stepsons, Gary Jr. and Dax, also live nearby, and her stepdaughters, Tina and Danielle, live in Phoenix.

Other books by Kim Schaefer

resources

For a list of other fine books from C&T Publishing, ask for a free catalog:

C&T Publishing, Inc.

P.O. Box 1456

Lafayette, CA 94549

(800) 284-1114

Email: ctinfo@ctpub.com

Website: www.ctpub.com

C&T Publishing's professional photography services are now available to the public. Visit us at www.ctmediaservices.com.

For quilting supplies:

Cotton Patch

1025 Brown Ave.

Lafayette, CA 94549

Store: (925) 284-1177

Mail order: (925) 283-7883

Email: CottonPa@aol.com

Website: www.quiltusa.com

Note: Fabrics used in the quilts shown may not be currently available, as fabric manufacturers keep most fabrics in print for only a short time.

Great Titles

from  C&T PUBLISHING

Quilted Garden Delights
Make Your Quilts Bloom—8 Quick Projects
Holly Knott & Diane Knott

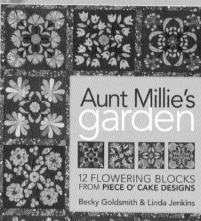

Aunt Millie's garden
12 FLOWERING BLOCKS FROM PIECE O' CAKE DESIGNS
Becky Goldsmith & Linda Jenkins

Carol Burniston
Color-Splashed QUILTS
FUSE FUN APPLIQUÉ TO YOUR PIECING

12 Quick Quilts & Playful Projects to Decorate Your Home
cute as a button Quilts
Joni Pike

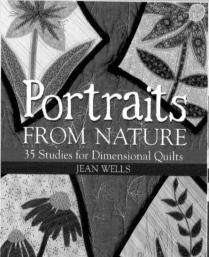

Portraits FROM NATURE
35 Studies for Dimensional Quilts
JEAN WELLS

Machine Appliqué Made Easy
JEAN WELLS
...ER'S GUIDE TO TECHNIQUES, STITCHES & DECORATIVE PROJECTS